He Lets the Stars be His Guide

by Jeffrey Schweitzer

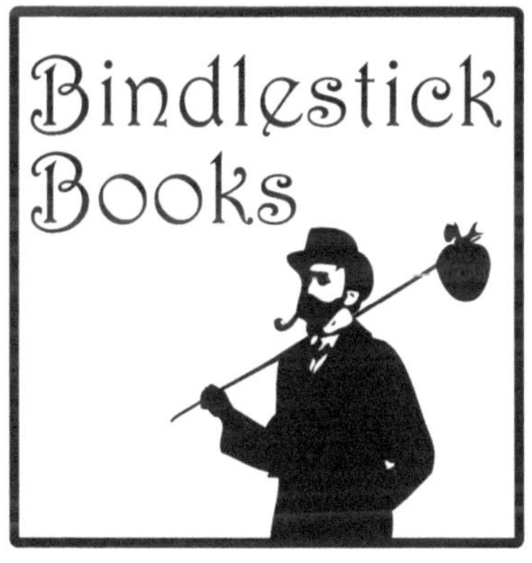

Bindlestick Books

Santa Fe, New Mexico

Published by
Bindlestick Books
Santa Fe, New Mexico

First edition.
ISBN: 979-8-218-10816-8

Through a foggy endless night

he chased the bright burning
light

of a thousand distant stars.

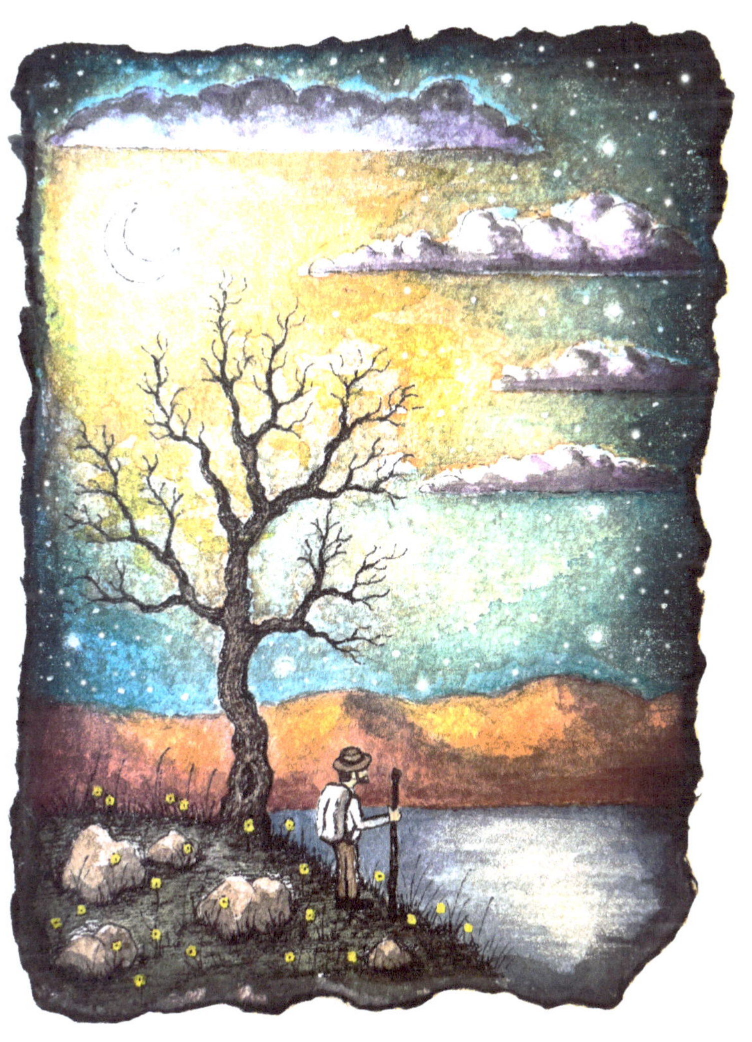

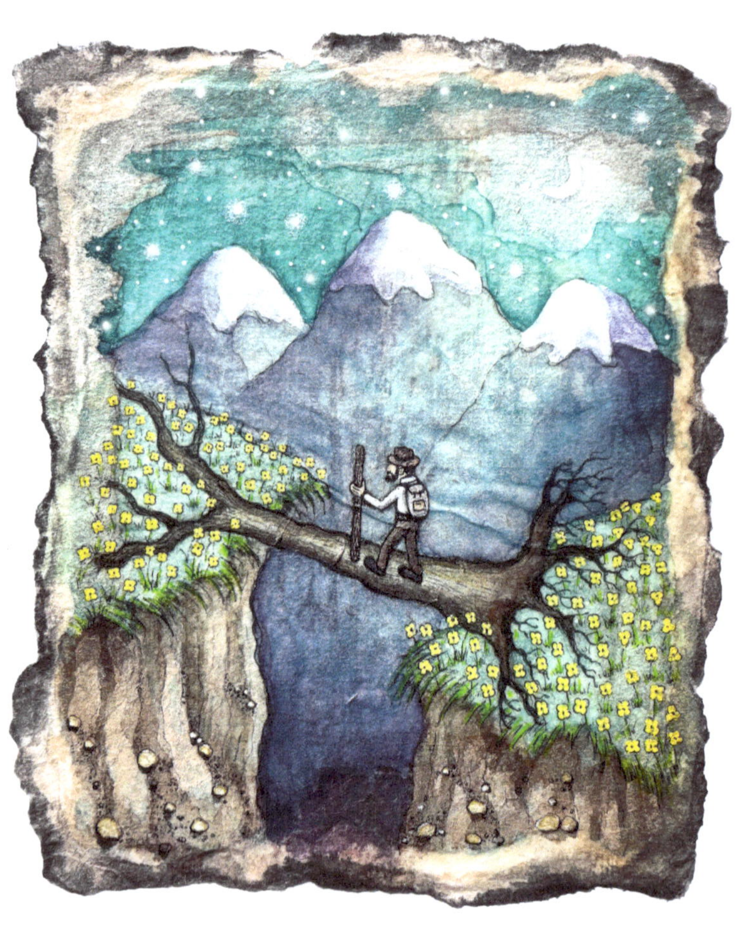

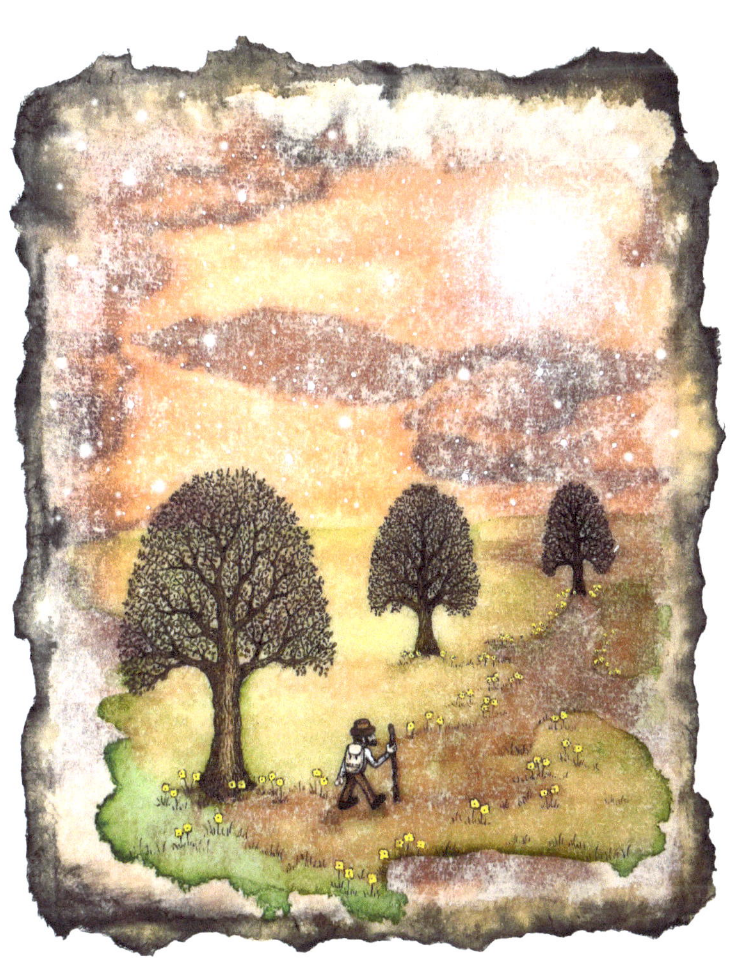

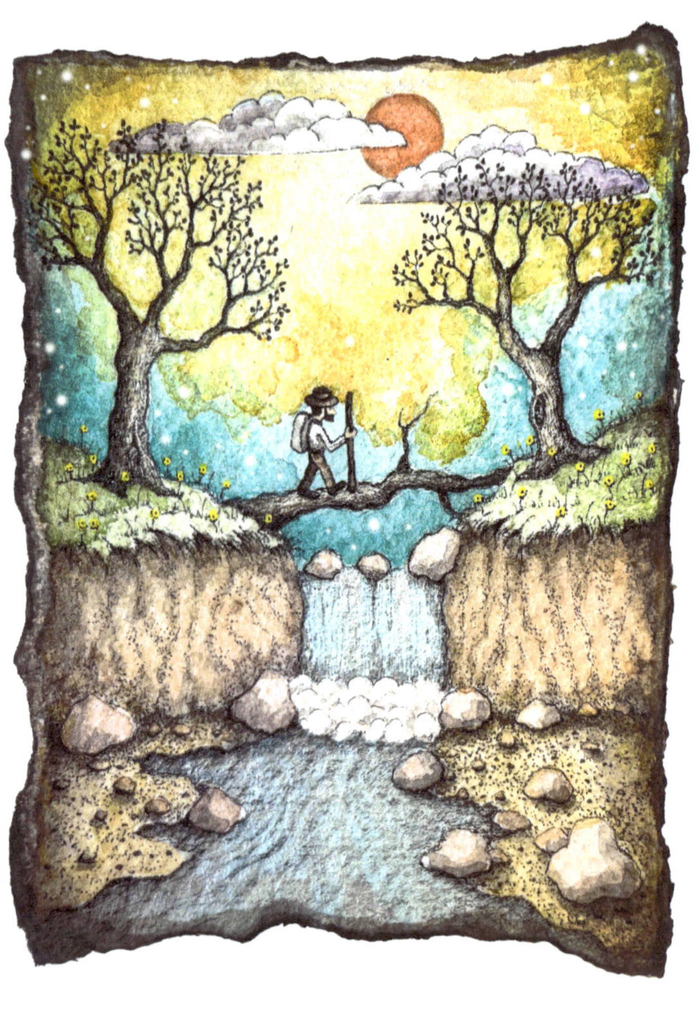

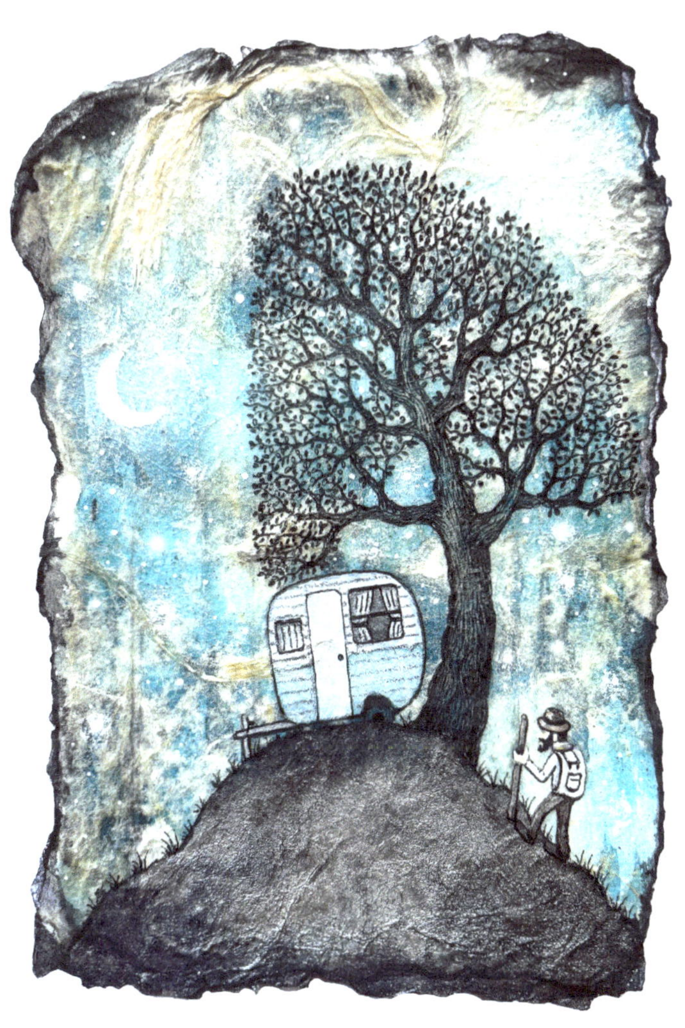

Each time it felt as if he
were getting closer

they would lazily drift off

mocking him.

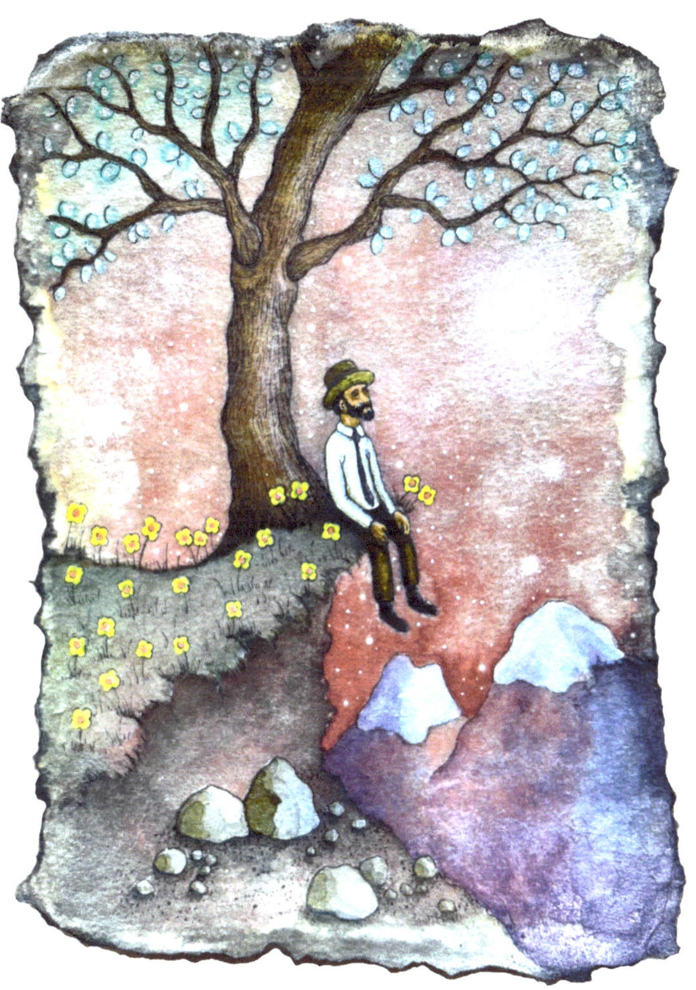

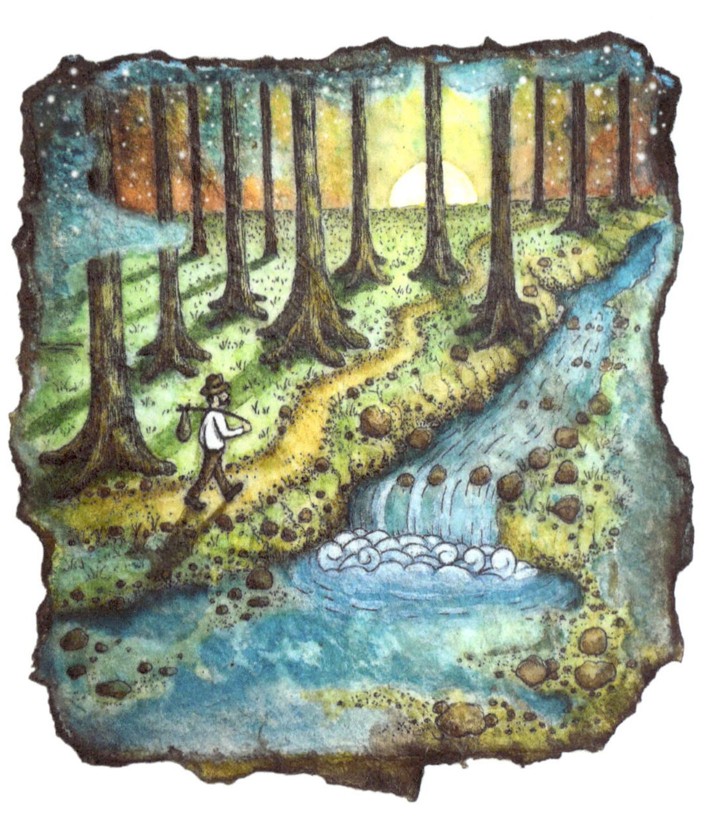

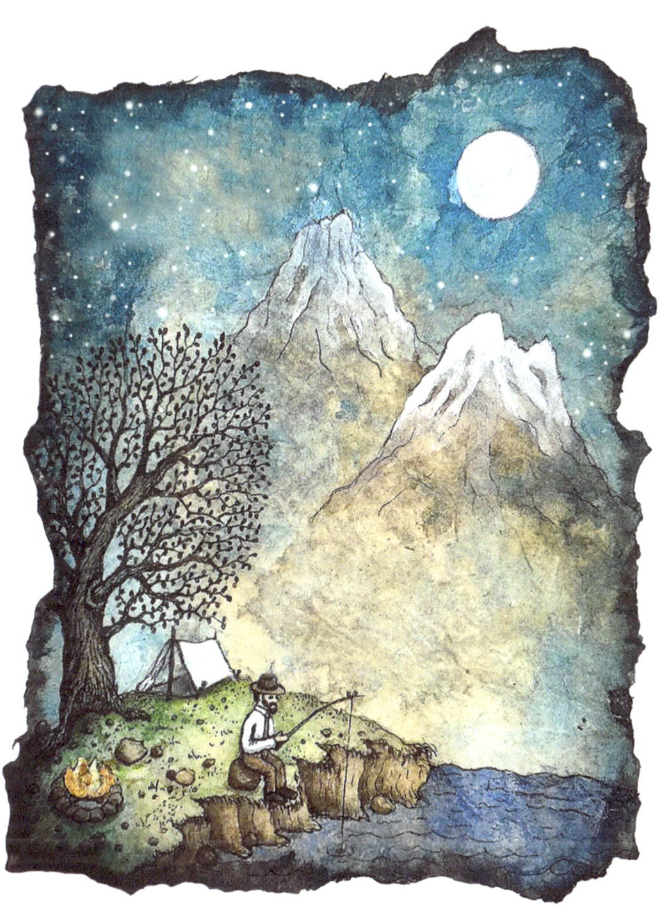

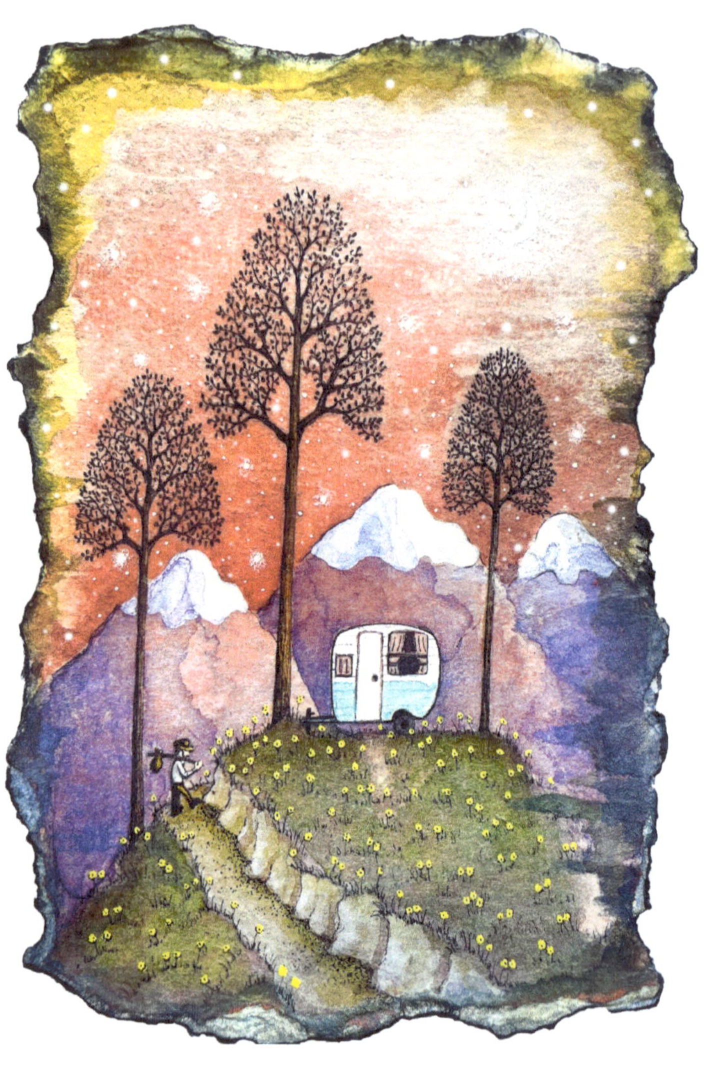

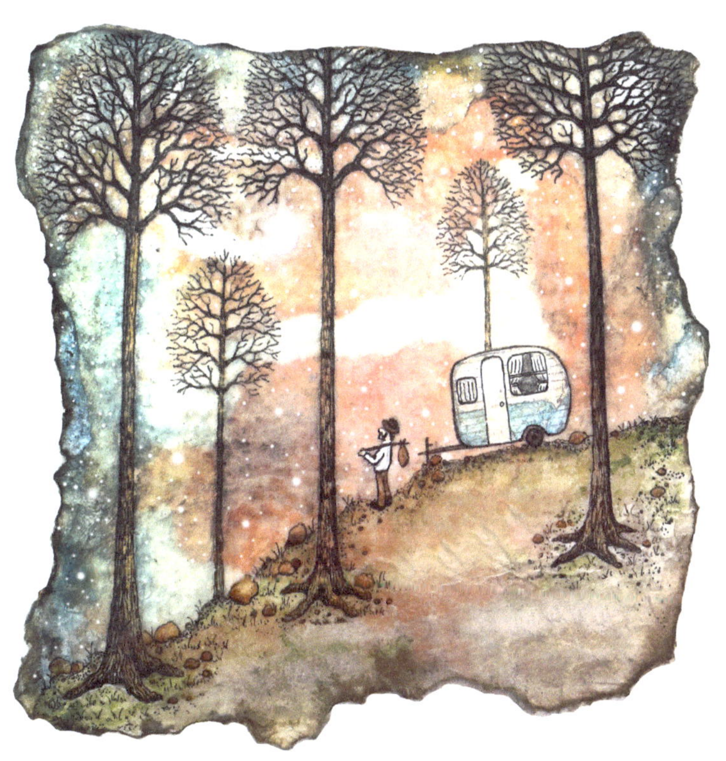

Just when they seemed within
reach.

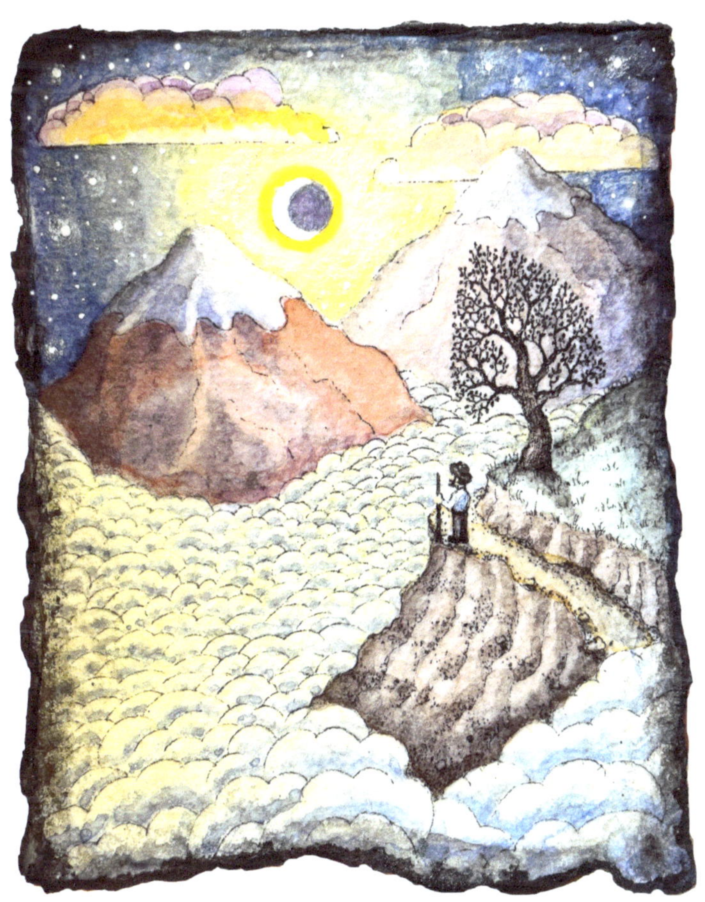

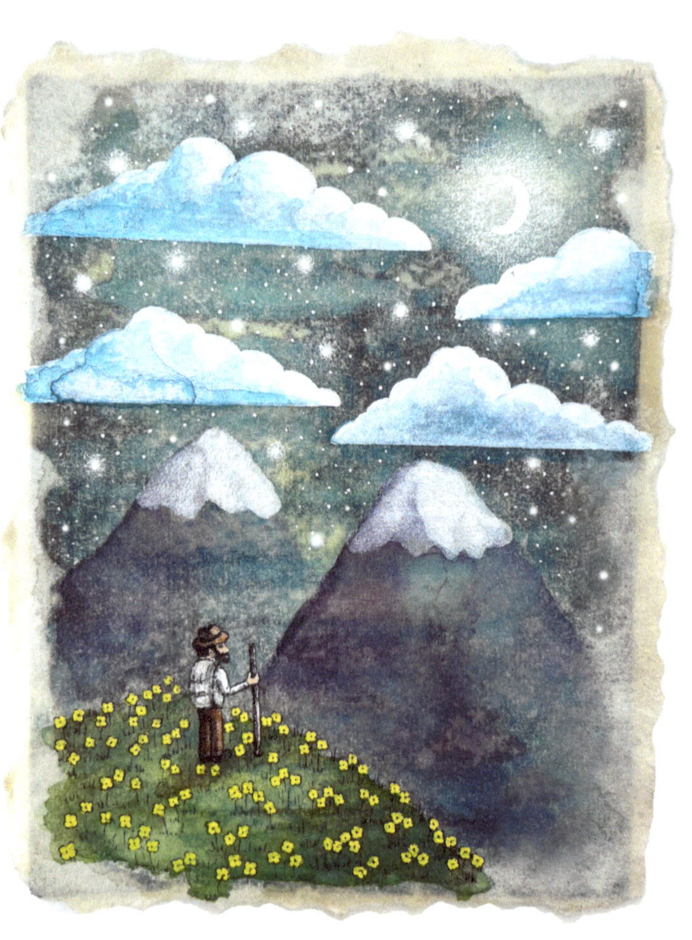

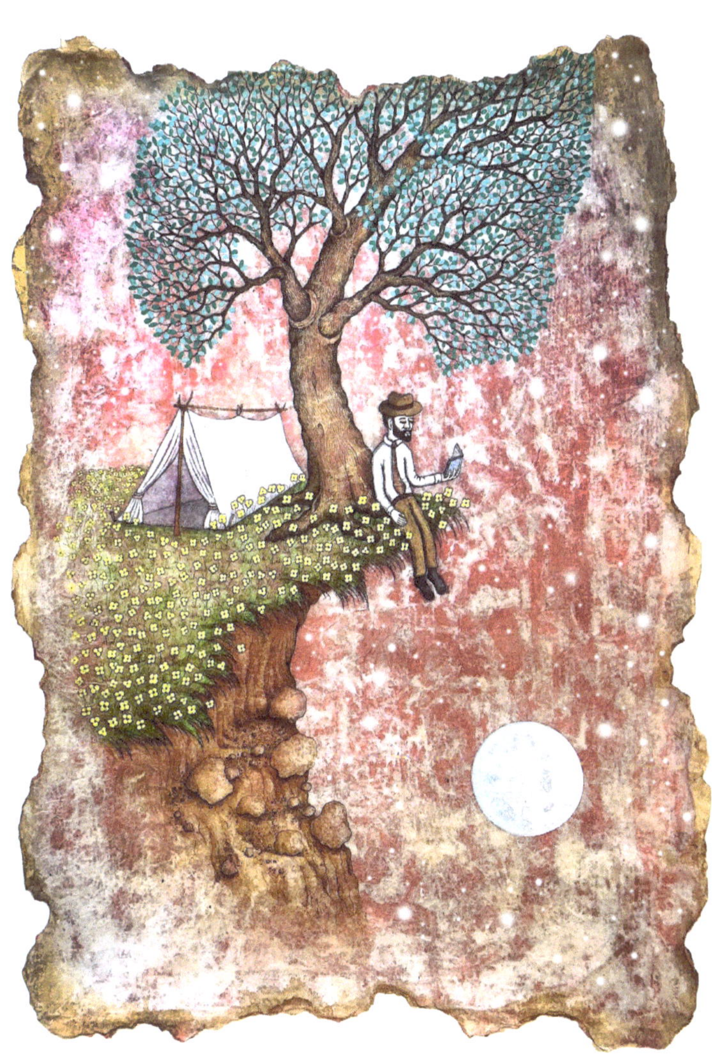

Some would fade away slowly

becoming barely visible

then disappear altogether.

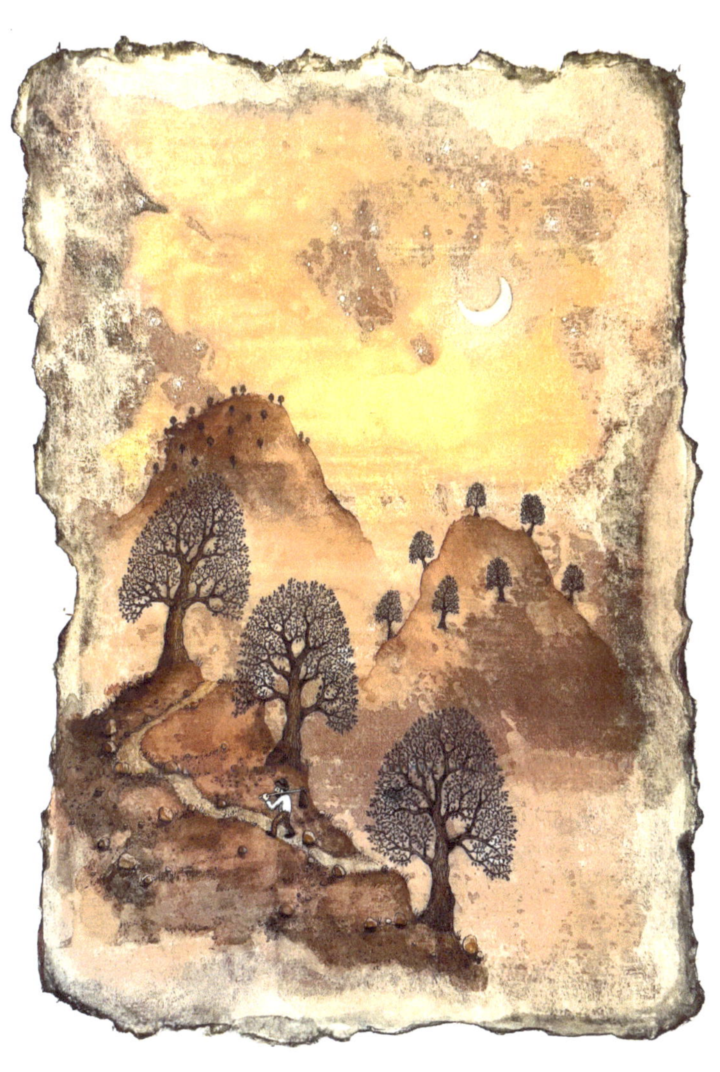

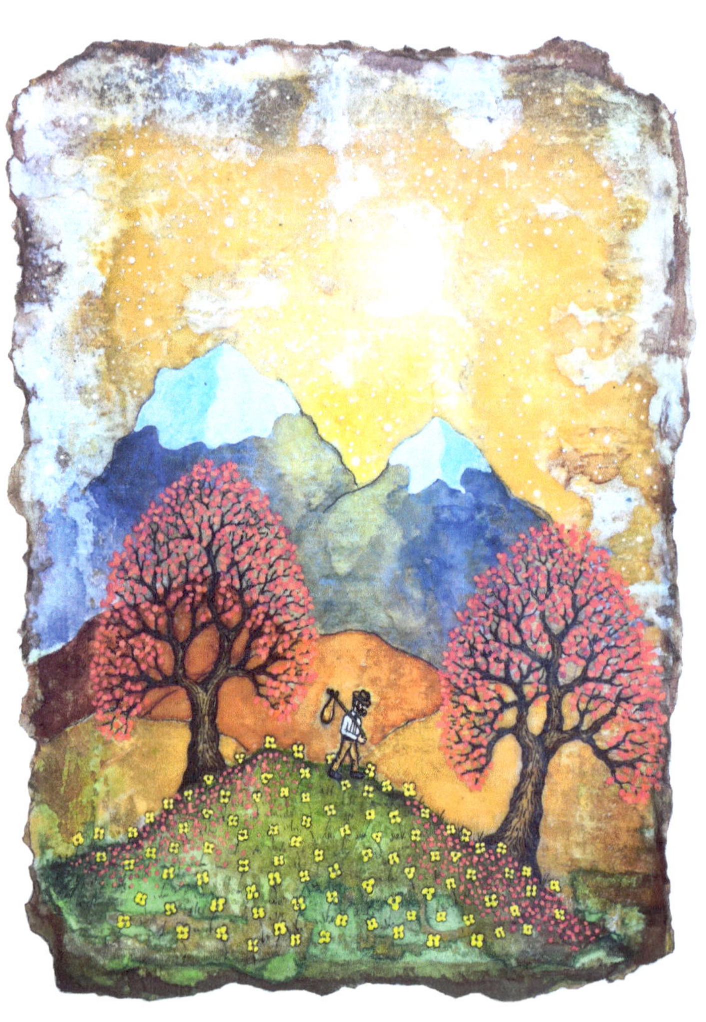

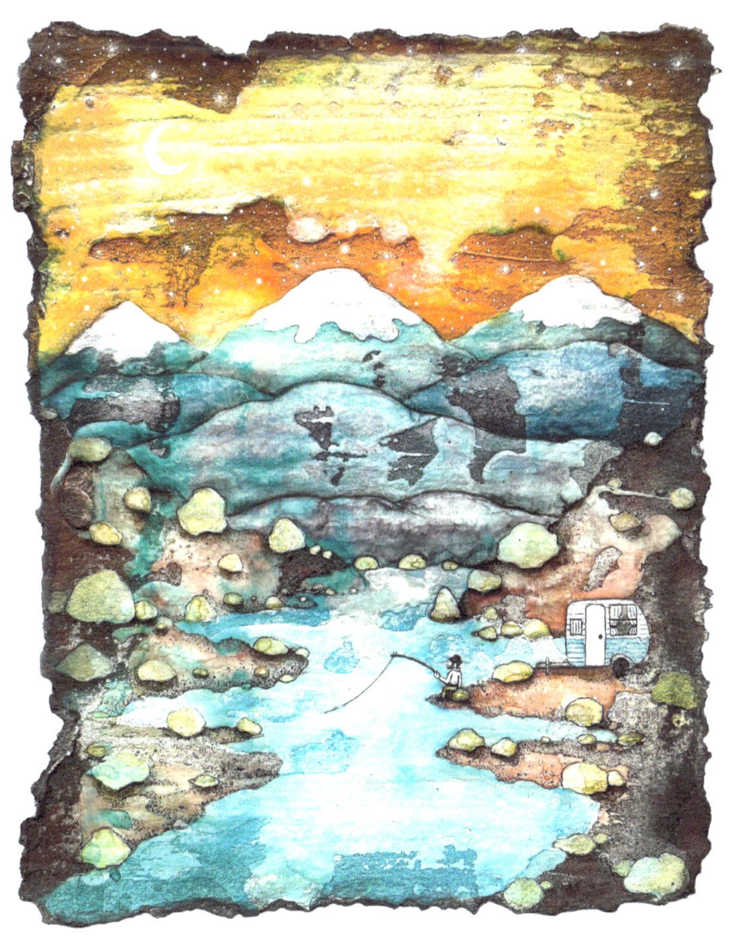

Others would grow increasingly
brighter

burning a brilliant white hot

that hurt his eyes to look at.

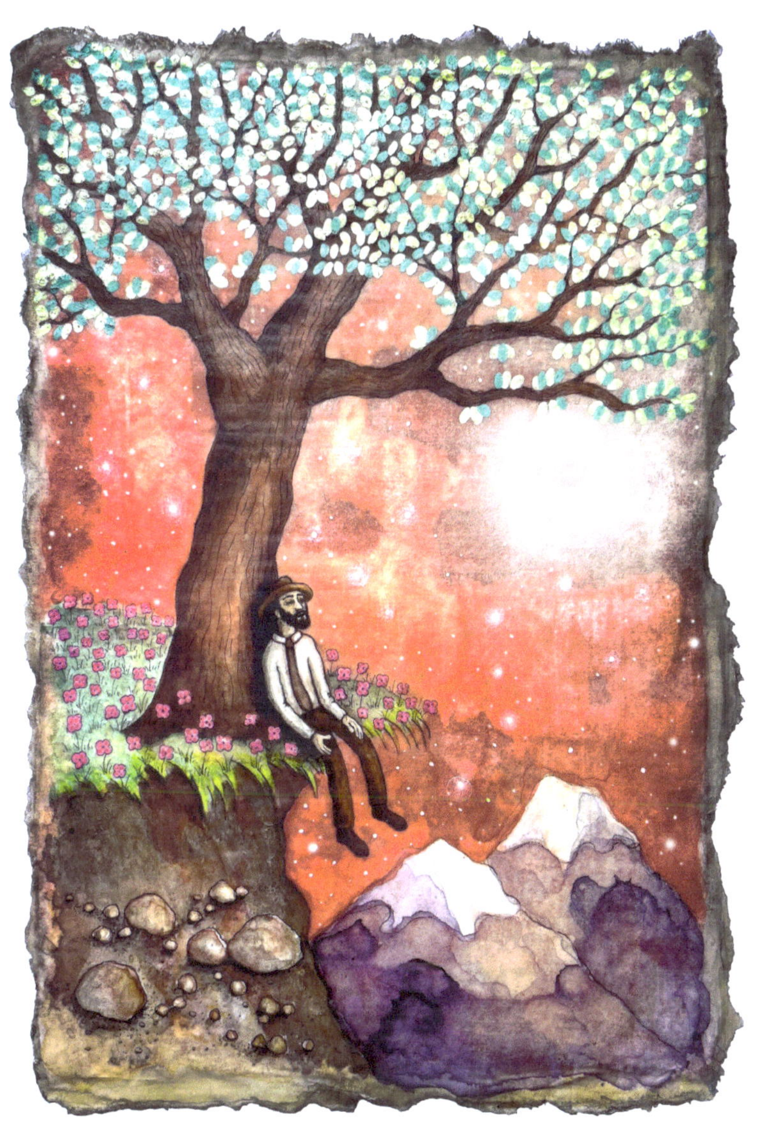

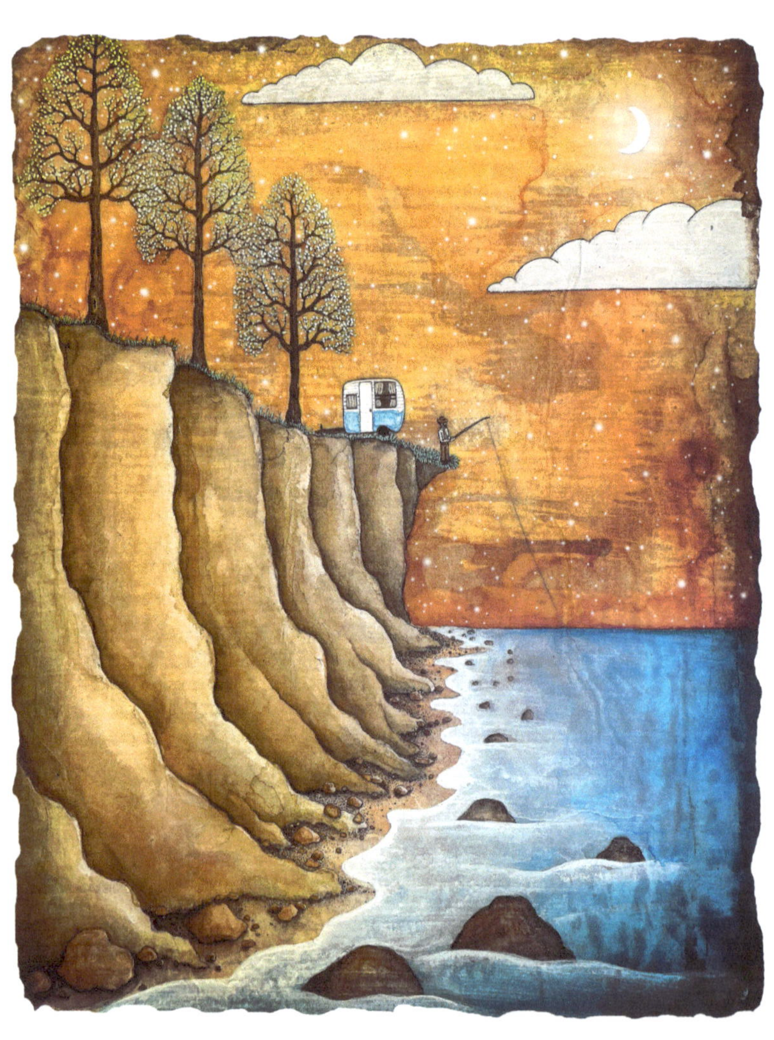

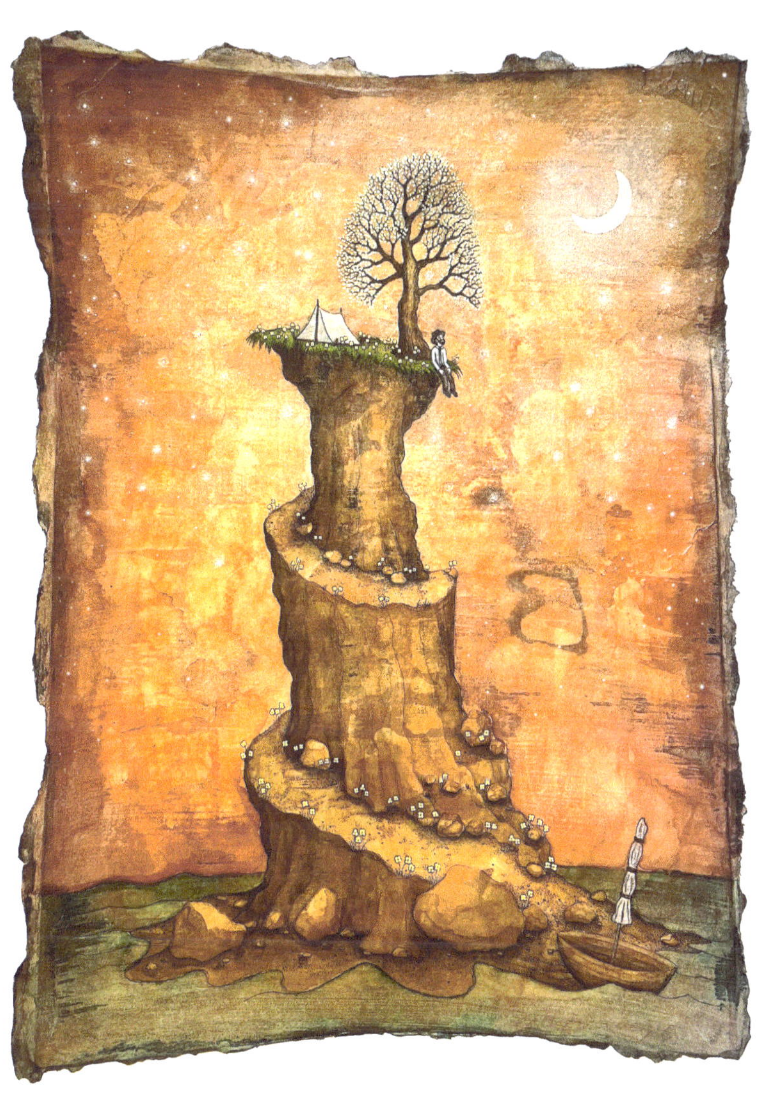

He could not look away

he kept moving

as did they.

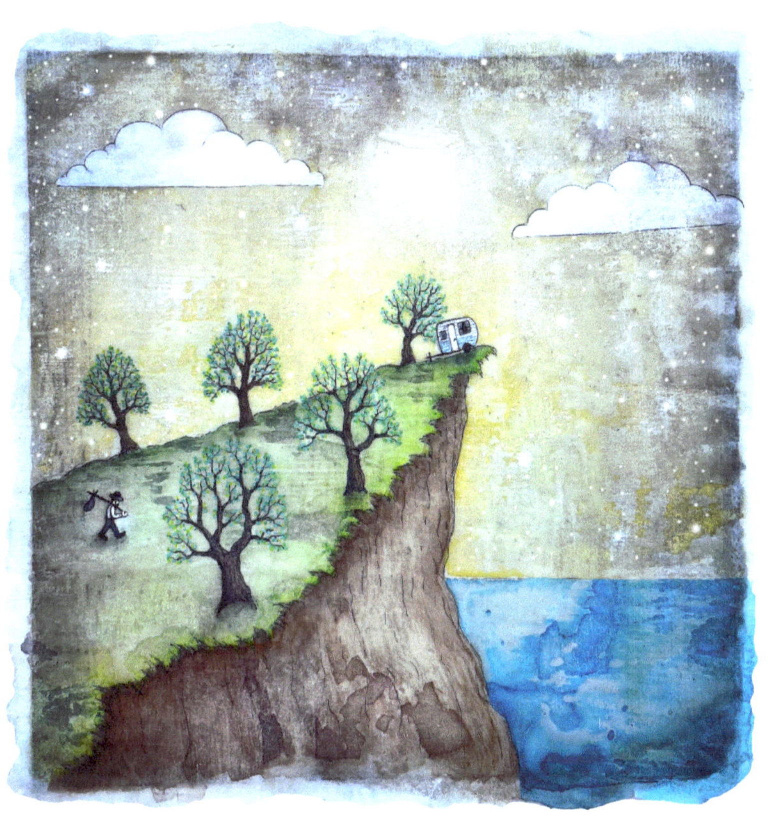

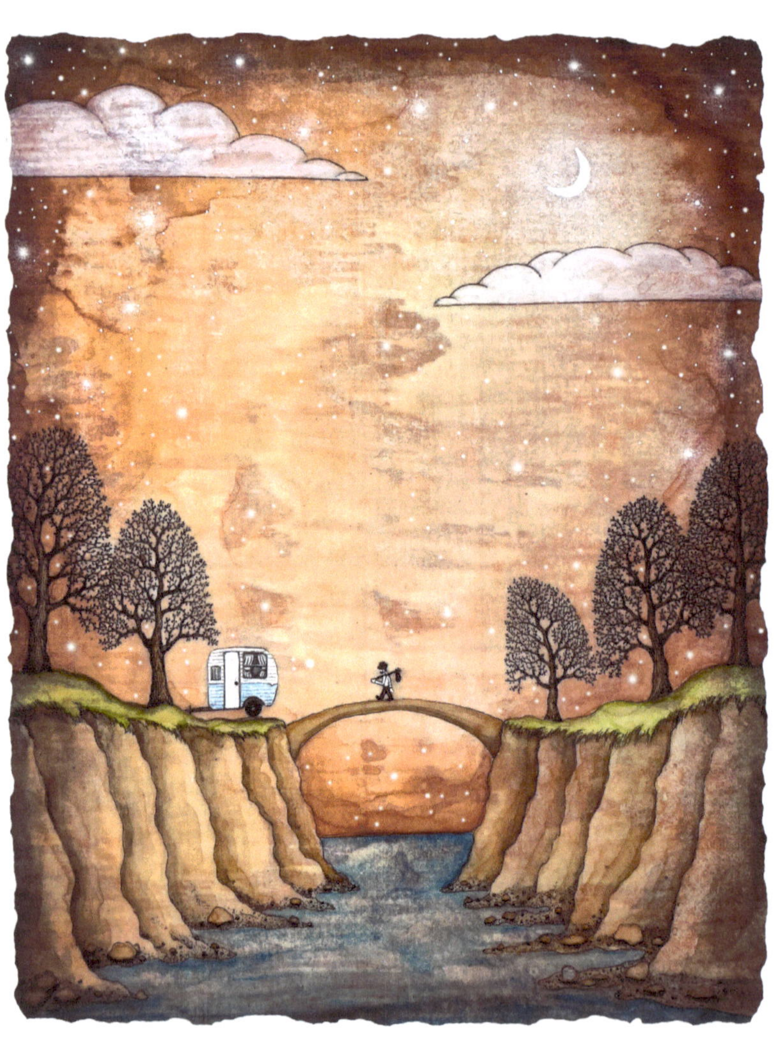

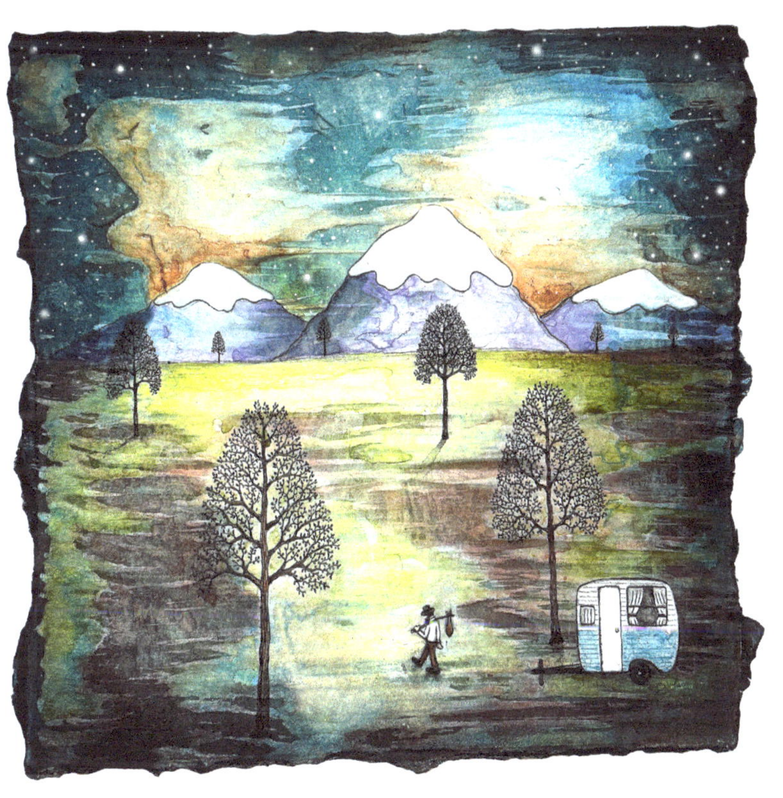

On more than one occasion

he feared

he may have been led astray.

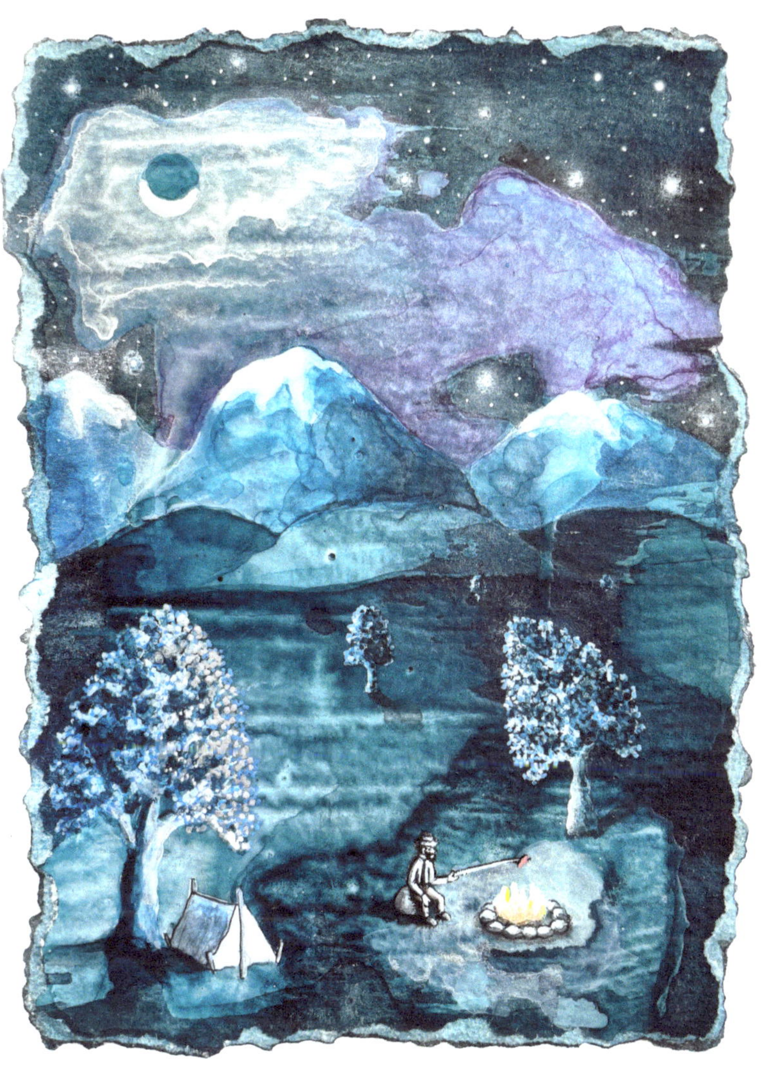

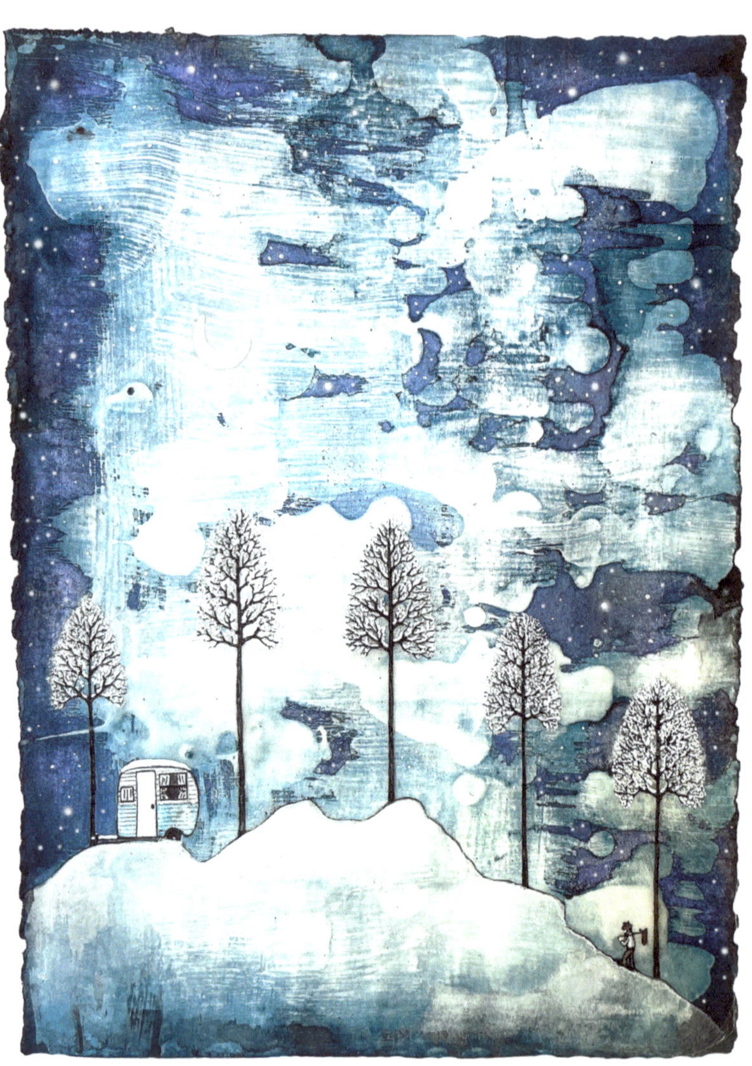

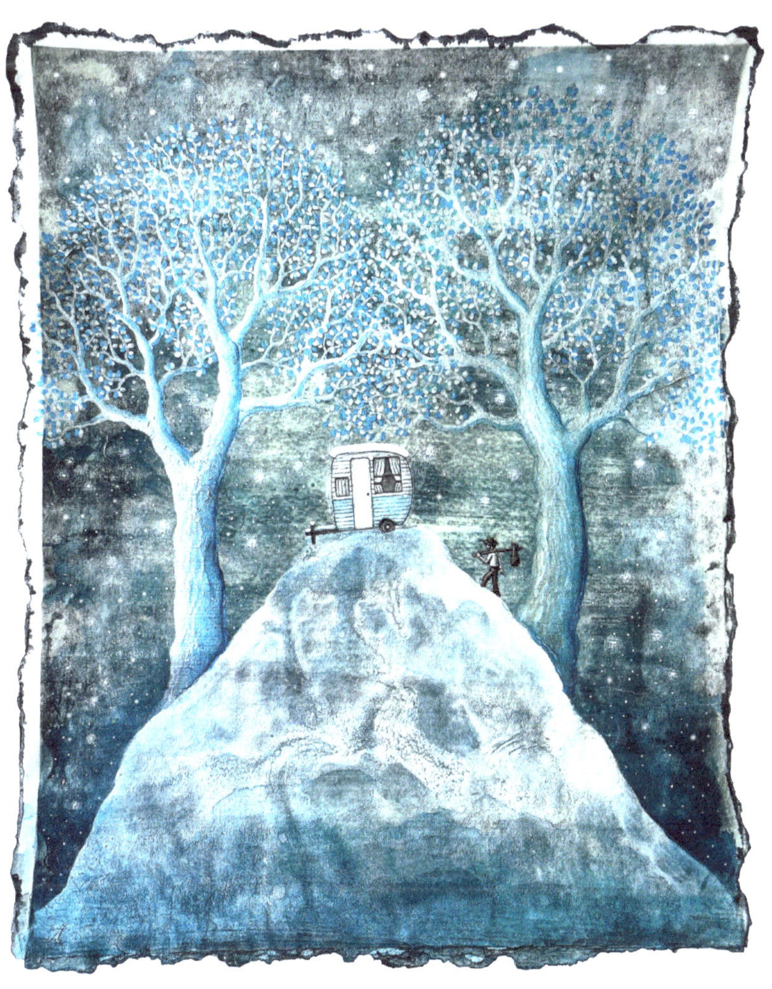

He would not go back.

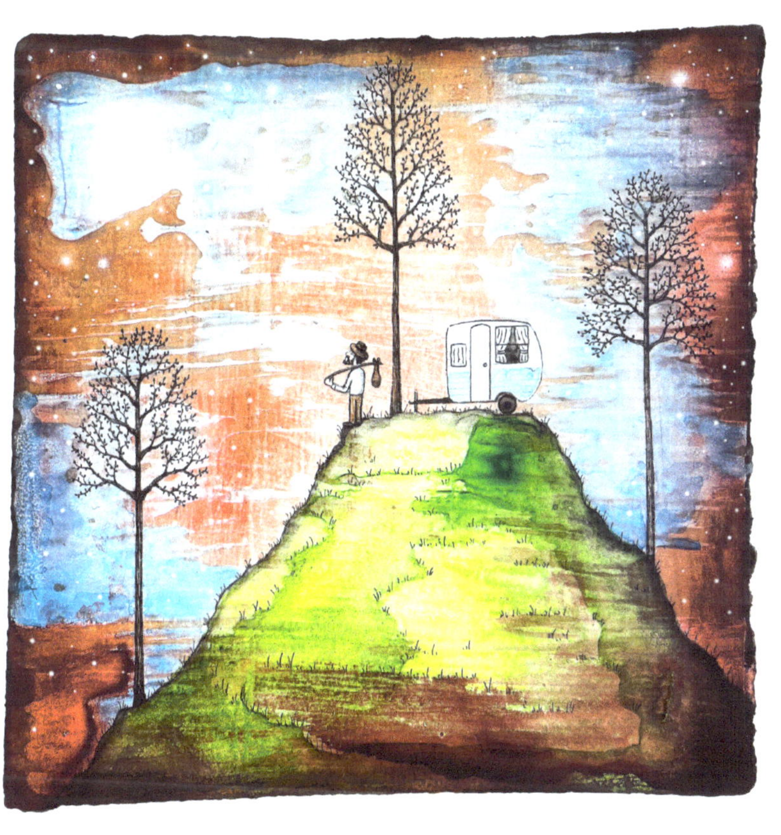

So he pressed on

chasing miracles

searching further and deeper
into the fog.

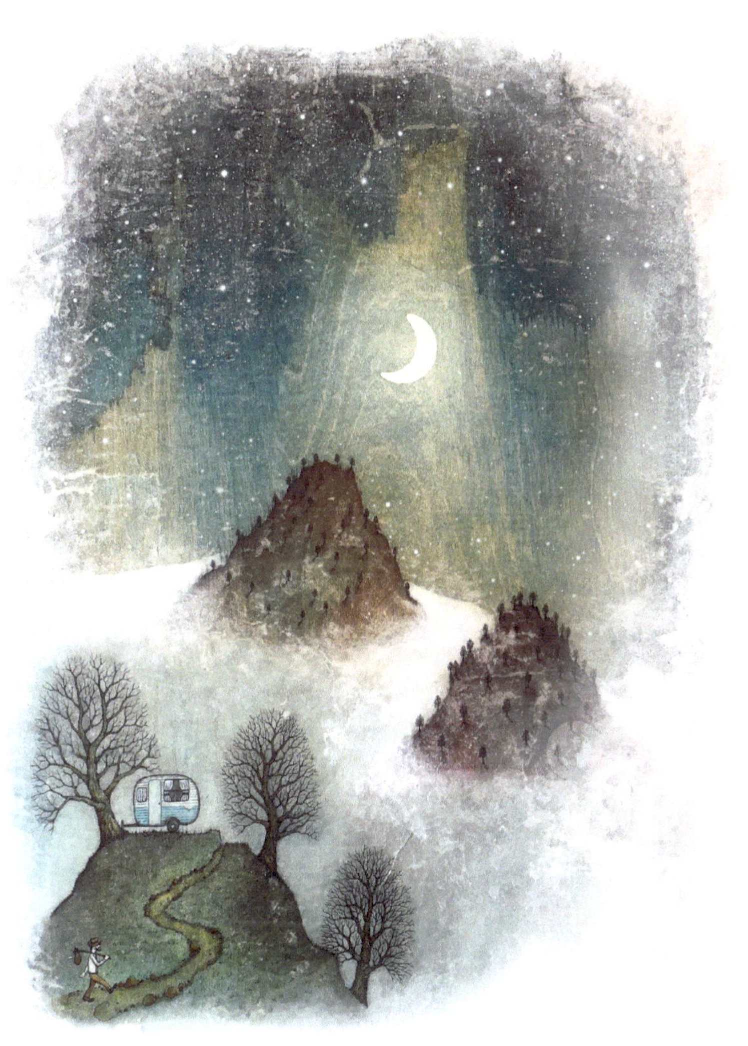

Books by Jeffrey Schweitzer.

Uphill and Into the Wind

He Lets the Stars be His Guide

Home: An Illustrated Journal

Countless Hours

The Mundane Ghost

Tales of Wizardly Whimsy

The Eccentric Gentleman

Into the Moonlight